14
Years

AuthorHouse™
1663 Liberty Drive
Bloomington, IN 47403
www.authorhouse.com
Phone: 1-800-839-8640

First published by AuthorHouse   07/15/2011

ISBN: 978-1-4634-2653-8 (sc)
ISBN: 978-1-4634-2652-1 (ebk)

Library of Congress Control Number: 2011911262

Printed in the United States of America

Any people depicted in stock imagery provided by Thinkstock are models, and such images are being used for illustrative purposes only.
Certain stock imagery © Thinkstock.

This book is printed on acid-free paper.

14
Years

JENNIFER MESKUN

authorHOUSE®

A Person

A person so closed off on the inside shattered in to a million pieces like a mirror thrown to the bathroom tile

A person who views themselves looking through that shattered mirror only wishing they liked what they saw on the other side all they see is something they wish they could change or improve upon

A person like a faucet so closed off to their littlest emotions that when they do let their feelings out they feel guilt that someone else will catch on to how they really feel and then they will be caught in their own web of destruction

A person with a thousand means but nowhere to go

Stuck in the middle of life with a million things beyond her control she wonders why her life always seem to follow the reflection of the haunting past

So confused she walks a fine line some day's she is a year into this but so days she sees no hope

The one thing that would complete her in her life seems to be her biggest obstacle everyone else has it but she keeps on waiting keeps looking in that mirror wondering what is wrong with her

As she looks around she wishes she sees she gets disturbed by the harsh reality of what isn't there and what she feels should be for every story she hears of mistreatment that is one more reason why she prays to god it will be her turn

She is shattered inside her heart is breaking but nobody knows or can even understand this feeling some days she feels like she walks or crawls this path more like a turtle all alone not knowing why or how but she knows and feels it is unfair but has to hold on its her dream

This is been the toughest decision of her life but yet the only thing she wants to wrap her mind around these days she has good and bad days and sometimes to be honest she does not think she could go another minute without an answer but she does she keeps going because she needs to know

Her heart sinks because she feels selfish for once in her life a person who has given everything to everyone but her happiness is no more her faith is dwindling in the breeze and her resentment and anger is on the forefront

She is not usually angry but at this point she feels she needs a miracle in her life something has to give one way or another her heart is so heavy she is longing to be something that so many others are good or bad they are but she has that calling she has had it all her life

What do you do when the reflection is staring back at you and the one thing you want more than anything in life you can't have? Where do you look? Where do you find the answer to that?

My Poems

It's not something I understand or can comprehend
These words just flow from my mind
Writing down every emotion letting it flow freely from my soul
Letting myself be inspired by where life's path takes me

It's a very private thing I don't let a lot of people into these
feelings I have
These words are the key to my soul the key to every waking
moment in my life
Only a few lucky souls know the real meaning of these poems

My heart and soul breathe these words to me day and night
I feel things so strongly I have the need to express them get
them out write them down
I write from my heart the images I see the words the feeling
it's my way of expressing every detail my mind has to offer
the audience

My soul comes out in a lot of my poem
This is personal experience I am reflecting upon
I am reaching to the depths of my being pouring out to you
the best of my intentions
It's a way of getting it all out saying what I need to say
emotionally emptying my soul

There are times in my life when all I do is writing
It helps me get through life's messes
I t helps me to understand myself and what is going on
inside my brain
My brain goes ninety miles an hour some days on an idea
and does not stop
Sometimes I can write a poem in my sleep
Or I could get up at three o clock in morning
Whatever I need to do I just get it on paper

I can be free to be me
I don't' have to talk to anyone
It' my own words know one is twisting them around
I can yell
I can scream
I can say whatever I want
It is my writings and I am in control

Model

Were not here to fit into a click were not here to fit your mode
We are here to serve a different purpose
You broke me down you tore my walls down
You saw who I was and got inside me and destroyed my
mechanics
You nitpicked my soul you ripped me to sheds what the hell
were you thinking?

Why did you turn the tables?
I trusted you for about a second till I realized who you really
were?

Janie

When we were born planted inside of us was a seed a seed so very special and yet so full of emotion. This seed would be a constant reminder of the pain endured the tears cried the disappointment felt and most often the feeling of never being good enough.

Emotional abuse hurts it's like your soul is being ripped out of your chest and thrown on the ground repeatedly being stomped on. Later on in life when someone hurts you again the cycle repeats itself. We never recover from being shattered of our real selves we develop this image that other then the abusers want us to be we aim to please but inside we are a delicate flower. We are like shattered glass pieces all broken up. My petals are wilted and falling off, like a harsh wind storm keeps beating them down again and again we are suffocating here we need some air are petals can become whole and begin to have the re growth we deserve. We need the re nurture the love the care and tenderness. These delicate flowers need to see the sun. the positive rays need to shine on us to wash away the painful scars left behind . . . our petals are once again damaged we have to prove ourselves again and again. That little seed inside of us is being replanted over and over again.

It's a process that many people don't understand that they choose to wash away and think we are the ones with the issue. They are the ones who can't heal they can't love they are incapable of happiness and their worst enemy is themselves and their jealously.

You can't do justice in this world today if you take the good people down to make yourself look good or feel better. Who are you to have earned that right? You better take a look around and figure out the world isn't a very nice place and what goes around comes around. It's also not your call to make these kinds of judgments calls about people when their time is up those are not your choices or decisions.

You may walk alone in this world but I never will. I have worked way too hard to let you ruin who I am as a person. This is me and I am never going to apologize for who I am, and I'm not changing for anyone. Don't take on something bigger then you can handle. It may be words to you but to me it's my heart my soul and my character you are destroying piece by piece wall by wall it's all falling apart. That's who I am fragile and sensitive but I am real and I live by principle how many people can say that?

Love

Love is everything you are and everything you mean to me
Love is this incredible feeling you get in the pit of your
stomach
Love is the deepest emotion you have ever felt
Love has no words to be said no words to explain you just
know that is all
Love can conquer the unconquerable
Love is the best feeling a feeling you can't explain it
Love is the smile in your heart
Love is passionate
Love is dedication
Love is devotion
Love can cure anything and everything
Love can save a soul and you saved my soul
Love can make all your dreams come true
Love is more than a word there is a deeper hidden meaning
behind it
Love is something that you can always count on
Love is when I look into your eyes I see it
Love is written all over your face everything you ever wanted
to tell me
Love is in my words they give me the strength to go on
powerful messages flow from my heart and soul
Love is in my words my words speak directly to your heart
and soul your mind and body you spirit is always with me
Love is you and I

Love is like a fairytale story
Love is so magical like snow falling
Love makes you want to run around in the rain and dance as
if you were still a child
Love makes you feel creative
Love clears all your senses
Love allows you to be who you are
Love accepts everything
Love is kisses and hugs tears and shrugs
Love never robs you of reality

Loving You

Loving you has been the best thing in my life
Learning about the real you has been second best
We have grown so close; it was true love at first sight

The last four months have been nothing but a fairytale
The last month has been a bit of a struggle
Loving you so much has its downfalls but most of the time
it's crazy love
Time sometimes stands in our way, and distance is just a pain
but I still love you all the same

Being in your arms is the best it is really love at our best
Kissing you is the rest of the test but nothing beats out love
like the true test
Making love to you is like better than before wanting you
every touch more and more
Feeling your heartbeat against mine gets me every time
Your touch your feel your caress you make me love you with
so much zest
You loving body against mine make my heart skip a beat
every time
Inside out without a doubt you give me no reason to pout

I love you forever that is a fact and noting will ever change that
A happiness that can't be described only a feeling or some
special vibe
Nothing in my life will ever remain the same and you are the
blame
You're my inspiration my reason for living and also for giving
A push a shove you're always there to care
Love support that is what you give 100% that is not a fib

Not only a best friend but someone who will be there to the end
A soon to be husband a hero it's all the same you are my life
and I am not ashamed
You were my angel send from above to capture my soul with
a special kind of love
A time in my life where I want nothing more than to be your
wife

I am going to miss you while you're a thousand miles away
and believe everyday and me I will be thinking of you each
You're my smile in my heart oh my god where do I start
You make me weak in the knees
You make my heart melt oh my without a doubt

Your sexy you're charming you're oh so alarming
Your smart and handsome I just feel like dancing
In your arms I feel so beautiful
You lift my spirits and my soul you just make me glow

Without a doubt loving you is the best it puts everything else
to the test
The real test is surviving the little bit of crying, the tears and
sorrow the saddened heart of tomorrow
Watching you leave make me want to be with you even more
But knowing I can't be there every time

Looking at my ring as you walk away
The shine the glare I just stare
I look I see and there you be
Your face so clear in my mind takes the pain away every time

Watching as you disappear, makes my eyes disappear makes
my eyes tear
As I tear myself away from your window I just stare
I am so attached that I just can't bear the thought of you not
being there

But as I understand you are in command of a job that's in
demand
You're doing it for the right reasons and for that I can
understand because you are the man to complete the job
You're sexy in uniform

When it's all said and done I love you a ton
Without you I would not have been won
With you I am and will always be your number one!!!

Choices

Not so sure what I would say anymore
The pain is still there but it no longer is a burden
I see right through you and your games
I have walked down this path with you before
It never makes sense to me and why would I start to think it
would make sense now

You could write volumes about you you're so complicated
You defiantly have not out grown those emotional issues
You are still not good about talking about your feelings
You hide so deep tucked in your little shell and your just
clamp up hoping it will all go away
You get depressed till it hurts so much inside you can't take it
anymore and then you don't know what to do to handle your
emotions
Until that moment in time you're emotionless
You could never let anyone love you friend or not because
you're so damn serious about yourself and life in general it's
hard to get you to smile about anything
I try so hard to be your friend but it's such an effort these
days and I am tired of trying

I feel like I have done something wrong like it's all me
But your know what I am tired of feeling that way
I don't think it's me at all
It's something inside of you that chooses to feel like this
You choose to hide yourself from the world know one else
can make you come out and show who you really are I see it
but I can't do a damn thing about it and maybe I am the only
one who had seen the real you

Why don't you grow up and stop playing these games? Why
can't you tell the truth? I think you know what it is but you're
afraid of rejection? You are so stubborn . . . who really knows
what's going on inside you? I could guess a thousand guesses
and still be wrong

Hey did you ever stop to think maybe it's not all about your
feelings being hurt I have feeling as well I can't just stop my
life for you we were so young we did not even know at the
time we can't change the past, and we can't change what
happen now but we can acknowledge that we have both
grown up and moved on with our lives.

Nobody said life was easy and there was always going to be
a bunch of what if's in life or did I make the right choices in
life but in the end you take the path you choose will be the
one that will lead you to all of life's answers you have been
searching for. There is no right or wrong in life . . . . JUST
CHIOICES

Judy

Sometimes in life we can't predict the unpredictable

Sometimes we cannot prepare for the situations that seem to come out of know where and slap us in the face

Sometimes we are forced to face decisions we are not ready to make or that are not easy to make

Sometimes we meet people who change our lives they never stop believing in you, they become your rock when you're stuck in the hardest place you have ever been in, they encourage you and tell you it's not you it's your situation they try to find the lesson in everything you tried to achieve

You know you have tried your hardest you have held on with all your heart the damndest you could. You were committed still you would never walk away from the job you love those kids you love it's your heart and soul it you. Your beautiful your soul is generous, your heart is golden on the inside, you are not a quitter and I know you are staying as long as you can for the safety for the children as long as I could but is it worth ripping your soul to pieces sacrificing your very existence of everything your about.

You are an amazing soul so much more capable of so much more . . . Don't let anyone ever tell you are not good enough. We know what it was like to be told we were not good enough. We are survivors!! Just look in the mirror soul sister let's make a change!

Unexpected Bliss

Upside down inside out
A whole new perspective for this side
Centering in on the world above
Looking around at the images so well defined

Here is society look at it run together
Look at the clues it provides for us to live in
And look how we take it and run with it
Look at how are passions are defined

When you walk by and smile are you smiling at the world
yourself or someone or just your thoughts? What are you
sharing with the world when you walk on by every day?
What are your promises to yourself? Are you holding on to
promises to other people?

Are you being you or are you making some sort of statement?
What are you standing beside yourself or a wall? What makes
you passionate about life? What makes your heart scream out
with unexpected bliss?

Freedom of Speech

We are walking on egg shells
We are taking deep breaths
We are holding on to our freedom
We are doing are best
We are hoping and praying
We are saving our selves
We are whisked away and hid on the shelf

We said are peace
Now we moved on
We voted we Stood
But the ground we stood on
Was defeated and fought
And ran upon was
United as one
In a speech that confirmed
To the rest of the nation
What we already learned

Now we can move on
And only hope for the best
Knowing our attitude will fill in the rest
We tried to win this one and only doing our best was what
we could do we did not fail this test
It took a nation to decide a to cast a vote no one told you
that's all she wrote

Commitment

Words flow off the page naturally they just speak to me
I hear a voice the same kind of voice I hear when I hear
The numerous things talking to me the butterfly, the radio,
the wood logs, the fruit in the grocery store, the john deer
tractor when I am mowing the lawn, and the family of frogs
and toads who live next to the house.

I try to fight it but being one with nature is all I have out
here so I have to learn to appreciate these two aces of land.
The sunroom I adore the loft that had become my safe haven
for writing a creating everything my mind has to offer these
days. I guess there is a purpose for being here in this house I
just have yet to figure that one out.

I am out of my comfort zone entirely . . . I went from living
in a brand new custom built house to a nice lived in 14 year
old but everything redone to now below standard renting . . .
all because of the Economy and a choice I decided to make.
I guess sometimes you just have to stick to your choices. No
matter what I did not want to have to sell a house every 3 to
4 years.

Sometimes in life there are going to be heartaches
disappointments happiness smiles laughter tears missing
people . . . and so much more all wrapped up in to one
persons soul it can cause a little bit of stress here and there.
What about picking up your whole life and saying see you
later I am moving on? It's good but at the same time it's bad?
You lose all your connections . . . you feel so lost and alone.

So miserable some days, some days you just want to cry and bitch to your heart's content but at the same time you know it won't help. You want to feel your place in this world but you feel so misplaced? I don't know where I fit in? Always moving? Always changing? Where is my home? Where do I belong? What is my place in life? What should I be doing? I feel like I am wasting time?

I feel like I have so much to offer this world . . . so much to give back so much creativity to give out and nobody will give me the chance. I just find it very frustrating to myself. I want to be known I want to get out there. I want to run my own business. It might be a cupcake, a craft, a wooden box gift idea, a greeting card business, maybe a little bit of everything . . . called itsy bitsy pieces of love. I am just going to run with something and its going to take off and do will and make people happy and feel emotions. Feel and see things the way I do. Maybe it will be the book paved I have half written who knows.

Whatever happened to having a dream Jenn? Whatever happened to your spirit your drive? Why because you had a few blows you want to give it all up? I don't think so that was never you before. You were always the fighter the survivor the one who was never willing to give up without a fight. That is one of the best attributes about you. You have got to find a way inside your mind frame to make this work for you.

When I take a look at myself from the inside out I see this girl who has always used writing as her escape. that was her way out her way to communicate with the outside world hoping that one day someone would hear what she would have to say whether it be by accident or her own doing. It seems like there is always so much I have wanted to say. I have just always felt my emotions so clearly I feel things so deeply so passionately they just roll right off of me. I could never talk to anyone they were always concerned with their own problems or arguing themselves deaf. So I decided I would be better heard by a piece of paper then a human being at that point. That was almost 14 years ago. Imagine that. A little girl and what she finds as her security blanket at that time was a piece of paper and a bunch of words she had been keeping inside for only god knows how long, Living the way she did she needed to provide herself with an out or she knows she was not going to make it through some of those long drawn out battles that lasted until the dawns of the mornings hours.

Looking back on that moment I am saddened not necessary by the heartache that I had to endure but the amount of pain that still comes out in my writings today about that. How my writings began. Those basics for them. That is a sad way for my talent to be hidden because that was my way out. That is all I knew. This is all I had to be safe was hiding behind a wall of my own true thoughts writing out word for word that is amazing to me.

That's What Real is

Thinking of you brings a smile to my face every day.
 A friendship with a strong bond for each other Memories
created that will last a lifetime

It's not about how you look or what you say it's about whom
you are that I care about so much
It's what's inside
It's about what is in your heart

I am always afraid to be loved but with you I am
I was afraid of falling for you the wrong way but you have
taught me and allowed me to understand there are certain
kinds of love
Its love that goes without saying, but never stops being
unconditional.

You have seen a girl with many sides. You have seen a girl
with less beautiful sides and you love me all the same.

You have seen the girl who would rather put other people
before herself because that is what makes her happy.

Masks

The fact that some people wear a mask is an interesting characteristic to me

People like to hide behind that to hide their true identity so they don't have to reveal who they truly are

People like to pretend they are something they are not

People like to pretend to be something they always wanted to be

Some people like to start over brand new and leave there past lives behind like a cloud of dust in the air

Some people need the mask to hold back the pain from getting it to their soul and burning a hole in it

Some people need it to cover the scars that no one can seem to take away from the battle of cancer war or attempts at suicide

Some people wear a mask to shut out there daily life they live just to be able to get through the day we all have masks people—the player, the sex addict, the shop alcoholic, the alcoholic, the pill popper, the perfectionist, the control freak . . . we all have something what do you mask out of your life?

Do you mask out the truth? Does the truth hurt? Does your heart lie? Does your mind lie?

Do you use your mask to lie?

Do you use your mask to love?

What else does your mask say about you?

Maybe you should look at your mask and see what you are who is truly behind it?

What happens if your remove the mask?

What are you afraid of?

What will we see?

What can you say behind a mask that you can't say to my face?

You have to face life sometimes don't you think it's about time?

Don't you want to know who you have hurt in the process or was that part of the game of the mask you don't have to see who you hurt?

Do you think pretending and putting your mask on is going to change what life has to offer you? Don't you think you're going to be just as miserable?

You can't just be calm knowing you don't need a mask but you're not happy with that you want everything you can't have sorry it does not work that way you have to be true to yourself first no masks

I lost myself trying to wear too many different masks and I am not about to wear any extra masks other than the ones I need . . . wife, nanny, aunt, daughter, sister, friend, that kind of thing.
You need to decided if you're going to wear the mask of someone who hides and pretend and just cares when the mask is convenient for you so you don't get hurt . . . which I said from the beginning or then un masked friend that I have given you the chance to be; if you can't handle that then go behind that mask and hide out like you do so well.

Wrong

Somehow I am always in the wrong
The conversation always comes back to me
And had to do with some type of Journey I had in my life

Don't you see it don't you understand that your only trying
to convince yourself you really know who I am
Don't you see I am different those are your words
Don't you see that I am incapable of making it in this real
world?
Don't you see that my life is falling apart at the seams just
like you said it would?
Don't you see that you're WRONG?

Don't you get it you are so wrong about me
Oh that is right you can't get past your Judgments about me
You think that I am this horrible person who does not know
what she is doing with her life
You like to blame me for the mistakes you made with me
You were never there never the way you should have been
Other People See this wonderful, loving, motivated girl who
has dreams and you see this girl who is so incapable of ever
making it on her own
Why am I so incapable because I have challenged you?
I have worked hard to get where I am and you don't even give
me any credit for it
You always point out my negative traits and you are never
proud of me

Jennifer Meskun

Frustration rings from my mind like everyday news
I can't even talk to you
I get to the point where I don't even want to talk to you
It almost becomes a chore to talk to you
I give you the benefit of the doubt but most of the time I get
shit on anyway so I figure what is the point

You need to look at your life not mine you need to fix the
things you screwed up yourself
You need to concentrate on the things that need your
attention and stop worrying about my life
I don't understand you for a moment's time everyday with
you it's a different story either way it's you putting me down
so at times I wonder why it's even worth bothering with you
You will all your negativity make me a stronger person and
motivated me to do everything that you said I would never
be able to do
You are such an unhappy person look at yourself in the
mirror sometime that should tell you all you ever needed and
wanted to know
You judge me constantly based on my decisions in life
You don't understand your own actions and you never will
You walk in a shadow of your own fears

War

A sacrifice made
A Hero Born
A protection of one's country
Many Personal commitments
Many personal sacrifices
A truth to real it hurts

Death is a reality it's real and an ugly tragedy
So many war heroes of the past and present have gone before us
So many people I know are in the military
Some have served in the Iraq one of the most dangerous
places on earth
It's an emotional issue
It's not an easy situation especially for those who are involved
It takes a type of person whether it is spouse, family member,
girlfriend, boyfriend, wife, or husband to be serving or to be
someone of a serving member.

Distracted

I love the fact that he knows that certain something
My favorite everything
I have many crazy layers
Uniquely qualified to take on your world
Never to sticky
Sometimes the truth hurts
Anxiety is a wasted Emotion
Comfort is the bottom line
Some of the most beautiful people in the world Love
He wants to
Love you

To: My True Friends

Intriguing mind
Only footsteps she has taken
Living proof of what can be done
Good and Bad times
Stressful life path but in time evolving to change
Windy roads of mystery but still a shinning ray of hope
laughter and joy can be heard but it just takes the right
person to understand what you really have been through
It takes a caring nature
Someone who you can inspire
You show people the light with just the right life experience
You have lots to share and spare
A caring nature
A peaceful mind but
A loving heart I noticed from the start
When the two of us hang out together were like the nuttiest
of girlfriends
So much laughter so much pride
We are like shinning starts in the sky
So many emotions flying high
You're someone who understands me
You see the real me
You allow my soul to be free
You fill a hole in my heart a sort of wonderful spout of
motherly ways
There's a reason I met you
And even if I don't know for sure now I know I will find out
later on down the road
Such a kind heart and soul you have

A great friend I'd wish to have
Believe in beauty because that is who you are
Bare your soul to the ones you trust but not your mind
A soul is your true self-true identity
Your mind is sacred
I see who you are
You have walked into a trustful and grateful person this time
You are living proof of what a person can withstand
emotionally and physically
Just the ingredients you have created in your life to become
successful
You found the recipe through your despicable triumphs
You are a unique person and a very sensible person
You are worth every struggle you have been through you have
me who cares a ton about you
When you feel down don't frown I will be around to cheer
you up!!
Thank you so much for everything you have done for me
You have helped me out more then you could imagine
You have given me the strength to go on I see you and it
inspires me in my own life
You are a strong woman with continued strength in life
You always find a way no matter what is going on for that I
will love you forever

Our Vows

Dreaming about the day I walk down the isle
I might feel like I am walking a mile
Its okay anything to see your smile

Dreaming about 3 and a half months away
Then it will be all real all-true
The biggest day of my life
We can finally make it official and become a family

It's a place I never pictured myself at 21 years of age
It's something I never even thought about before
It' wasn't in the plans
It was just a twist of faith

The best feeling is to think my husband will be there to see
me graduate
My number one fan and biggest support for that degree
Husband something I never thought I would be saying
sounds so good

It's about starting out life together
It's about making our love last forever
It's about writing our vows

I Love You Because . . .

I love you because you're special
I love you because you're you
And I love you for everything you do

I love you because your one of a kind and your all mine
I love you because your true and you always make me feel
better when I am blue
I love you because you put up with my moods and you buy
my favorite foods
I love you because you're funny and you're good with money

I love you because you're my baby and you're defiantly not shady
I love you because you smile and you go the extra mile
I love you because your great and you're my #1 date
I love your because you're a man and my #1 fan
I love you because you're my inspiration and we can talk
about constipation

I love you because you're a pleasure but you're also my
number one treasure
I love you because you're modest and you recognize I am
your goddess
I love you because your sweet and I know you will never cheat
I love you because you're cute and I never want to put you on
mute

I love you because your fun and you have great buns
I love you because you're happy and you can be a little sappy
I love you because your mine and you oh so fine
I love you because you run and you are my little Hun
I love you because you're a hunk and I'm your little punk

I love you because you my little ball of joy and sometimes my
toy
I love you because your eyes smile and you never change the
dial
I love you because you've sailed a ship and never had a fit
I love you because you're fit and you always give a bit

I love you because you send me roses and do all these
different poses
I love you because you smell and you never dwell
I love you because you go to the mall and you're not 10 feet tall

I love you because you're a star and you come so far
I love you because your favorite color is blue and mine too
I love you because we fight but they were all right
I love you because you're mean and you run like a machine

I love you because you're my shining star and I can see you far
I love you because you're crazy and you are never lazy
I love you when you mad it makes me glad
I love you when you're sad it makes me feel bad

I love you when you're sick and you will never be a prick
I love you when you shy it makes me want to cry
I love you when your tasty it makes me feel hasty
I love you when your strong it makes me feel all gone
I love you when you run it makes me feel fun

I loved you when we met because you made sweat
I love you when you give me butterflies
I love when we make love I feel as free as a dove
I love it when you play I could watch you all day
I love it when you have fun it makes me want to run

I love it when I play it could make me drip all day
I love it when you kiss me it makes me feel frisky
I love to feel you up and down it make me want to wear a crown

Gloria

So full of life and a smile so bright
Eyes full of hope and promise
A very smart two years old
A precious face
Cute as a button
Brings so much joy to those around her
She is the little angel in my eye
The warm fuzzy in my heart
She is the shinny sparkle of my smile
There is a little devil in her soul you can see it in her eyes
She is such a doll
Most of all she is my little ball of joy

Its About!

I am so in love with you
It's about the simple things and nothing more
I am so lucky to have someone care about me as much as you do
You are willing to go out of your way to see me happy

It's about the heartfelt letters
It's about the calls to say I love you
It's about the emails of unconditional love and support

It's about walking down the aisle and making it official
It's about having you as a husband and the man of my dreams
It's about spending the rest of my life with you

It's about the smiles that go on for miles
It's about the endless nights of conversation
It's about the love we share for each other
It's about the dreams we share

It's about the kisses and hugs
It's sometimes about making love
It's about sending flowers
And sharing all your magical powers

It's about the sentimental moments we share
It's about the continuous moments when I need you there
It's about supporting the one you love
It's about being there for the worst of situations

It's about a lending ear
A helping hand
A loving heart and an open mind

It's about holding my hair back when I puke
It's about picking my eye buggies
It's about sucking on my toes
It's about picking my buggies
It's about letting me cry on your shoulder
It's about winning your heart over

It's about buying my favorite groceries
It's about spoiling me
It's about holding my hand
It's about kissing me in public
It's about going on a date with me
It's about not taking no for an answer

It's about loving me for me
It's about not being ashamed of me
It's about taking a risk
It's about being scared
It's about the joy and laughter
It's about the tears and sacred fears

It's about how you make my heart go pitter-patter
It about how you make my earth shatter
It's about being the sparkle in my eye
It's about being my Guardian Angel in the sky

It's about the effort you make
It's about not being fake
It's about the feelings for me
It's about making it though the rough times
It's about solving problems

Connections From Within

A lost soul so broken so hurt searching for answers

Looking for the answers in the sky written above the answers from god a sign a symbol something to hold on to

I feel so emotional so connected to you . . . I feel the pain . . . the not wanting you to be there alone in life right now where u are . . . don't give up we have been here before

This is much harder than anything you have gone through before I feel it but it affecting you so much more now your sleep your health your mental state. You mind needs to rest your heart needs to heal. You need to put yourself your health and your creativity first

You are in a very fragile state of mind and early detection for scars and trauma to heal is going to come first you're going to have to look in the mirror what do you see? I see a Delicate Flower who has lost all of her sparkle all of her shine. She is searching within to find the meaning of life the meaning of why she is still here. Why she is going through all this pain and guilt and turmoil for what? What is this supposed to be teaching you? The pain is over whelming you just sit and stare at the world wondering what is the purpose is? You have so much but you fighting with yourself to understand the rest.

You know what the principle is you get that. You may be one of the few in this world who has principle. It's frustrating out there so much talent but people just throw it back in your face and stomp all over the pride that we thought we had built back up.

We ask ourselves the question everyday will we ever be good enough for anything. I mean what can we do if nobody wants a piece of what we want to so badly give. Then there is always that fulfillment . . . always a need a void never met

A Grandfather's Love

A Grandfather loves so special there is no other kind of love like it
An Amazing man of many great words and talents
A man so skilled in fixing things he intrigued us all with his knowledge
A Man of great pride
A man who knows what hard work was
A man who gave up the dream of becoming a dentist to provide for his family
A journey of life so wonderful for others who did not know him knew he was a special guy

He was and will always be a true inspiration to me
In my mind he is nothing less than a true hero
He was a fighter no doubt, he had so much strength he, was one of the bravest people I knew
He never looked at the negative side of things he took his situation and made the best of it; it takes real courage and determination to do what he did
He had so much to live for and in the end he could not go on when he could not fight anymore he knew it was his time to close his eyes and begin again in a comforting place

He was a grandfather who has help build who I am today
He was a major motivator for me he taught me what life
was really all about, he told me not to give up to just keep
plugging away and I would eventually get to a place where I
needed to be
He also taught me that some people are so lucky; he taught
me some real good life lessons. He taught me that you
needed to work hard to get what you wanted and I have
never forgotten that, and that education was the key to your
future.
He also had faith in me and believed I could achieve
anything I put my mind to he still knows I can make it no
problem he is my angel guiding me from heaven
I have always admired him and I wished that if I could be
anyone in the world I would want to be him. I would want
to be remember for the person he was and still is today.

Cancer

Such a dirty word
A word that consumes more than your body it consumes
your mind
A word that is dreaded that no one wants to hear
It takes souls and matters into its own hands
How do you deal with something like that?

I have a feeling my journey has only begun
The process to not being angry with God
And the long process to healing my soul begins
It's not easy being your biggest inspiration to let go of
How do you make a decision based on the information given
to you?

The painful unforgiving slow process of Cancer
It just eats away at you little by little piece by piece
What I want to know is why all the good people get it.
Now its terminal not something there is a cure for

You think to yourself why? How could this be?
While you're thinking what to do the rest of the family is in
denial
Then you realize you need to pick up the pieces and so does
the rest of the family
You have to pull yourself together to have the strength for the
other person
You often wonder to yourself where do you draw the line?
When do you become whole again? When does the regret
stop? When do you stop asking yourself questions?

Jennifer Meskun

Do you know how to be strong?
But then you realize stop being selfish this person has build
you to be who you are
They have been your motivator, and inspiration
They have built their own legacy in you
So now you need the strength to live on and go on
They would want you to be happy they know you can
withstand a lot of pain

$\mathscr{S}$*uicide*

It took another life
A life consumed by the sorrows of life that no one even knew
about
Only a sixth sense told me something was wrong till I pieced
it all together
It's a form of pain many don't understand
It's a pain so deep so troubling they see it as no other way out
They hide a pain from everyone and everything in front of
them they keep going till there live spins out of control
They feel so isolated like they are crying out for help but no
one hears them
The drug the alcohol the emotional abuse the over the
counter pills the knife they may have become the only friend
you have in life
They walk a fine line of sadness grief anger hurt they are
untouchable almost soulless they don't know who they are
anymore they have abandoned everything and everyone they
know
They pretend everything is normal but they really hate life
but most of all they hate themselves and the fact that they
seem to disappoint and upset everyone
They walk in a shadow of their own fears
They see their guilt written all over the place and it
eventually eats away at their already precious mind
There is no easy button they can just push they just feel
helpless worthless until one day they can't take it anymore
and they end it all
They think it's for the best at the time but they never think
about the actual consequences they never think how it will

affect the people they leave behind, the unanswered question especially why?

The emptiness you feel the hole that is never filled you never stop thinking about that person or the decision they made that affect your life so much but in your life it's like the silent elephant know one talks about it they just go about their daily lives

Another wasted life over suicide another life shattered another family ruined another story never told another bright future gone taken so soon . . . but are we any more aware of the signs now then when you were alive?

The Message

The paper on the desk, the hand moving,
The thoughts flowing, the phone ringing the,
Machine picks up, clock ticking, minutes passing, eyes concentrating.
She looks up, the sun shines brightly in the window the
breeze blows the temperature rises and falls.

The computer on the desk is typing away, the night
Is falling the stars our shinning, the face in her mind
Is so real but the name is nonexistent. A light is turned on by
the flick of a switch,
It all comes to mind, the pen the paper, the notebook, in the
file cabinet buried beneath the books

The white out smeared across the folder, smelling of strong
perfume,
The emptiness of the paper seems to be unreal,
Everything is stuck together with glue the paper clips have
been removed.

If only she could see the note
The copier is empty the trash is gone,
What will happen to the letter that needs to be received in
the mailbox on the counter?

The empty chocolate cake plate,
Remains on the desk, she yawns and turns out the lamp,
Slowly sitting down she proceeds to keep turning on the
music letting it blare in the back ground.

She pictures in her mind recent snap shots of her and him
sitting on the couch laughing and she pictures his caressing
hand over her sweet soft pink lips
She see images of things going so right in her mind
everything went according to the plan she had drawn out
she saw the interest on his face the love in his eyes she could
remember the night he told her he loved her and nothing
would ever change that
Now snapping back to reality by a loud thud heard on
the stereo she remember sadly when they used to be so
happy, or she thought they were . . . but she clams up just
thinking about it now she wanted to tell him something . . .
something in that message
The message that was on the machine when the phone was
ringing that she never picked up

Dream State

I remember dreaming the most incredible dream
It was endless, kind of childish too.
The waterfall was so soothing as it fell down in sheets,
The wind was so peaceful, it sounded like a whisper in my ears.

Looking up at the sky and seeing the clouds
Big and puffy white in color, in my mind
I would have compared them to look like marshmallows

The rainbow shimmering, sparkling as every color was formed
Red, orange, yellow, green, blue, and violet.
The visions it brought to my mind me as a child trying to
run in the field to find the end of the rainbow, I wanted that
pot of gold so bad.

It was mystical and magical and at the same time even a little
distorted
The details of my dreams clashed but in my mind I just felt
pure happiness

The stars began to fall on the night sky
Looking at the first one making a wish,
My very favorite wish of all hoping and praying for the life of
me it would come true

Jennifer Meskun

Seeing things so clearly I began to feel compassion
To feel complete, it made me think back to the memories I
had as a child,
It brought back the obsession I had running through the
waterfall or kissing my one true love.
I thought it was romantic, living in some fantasy world I
would guess.

As the dream ended I remember feeling of well being
A smile of self assurance
A feeling that finally I accepted the truth
I accepted the person I had become today, and the
individualism I had just created for myself in the state of
mind I was dreaming in.

Rain

The rain fell upon my face,
The breeze as I look out the window
Seems to be getting faster stronger.

A little light has broken through,
But there is still a dusting of dark clouds
In the sky, can you feel the dampness in the air it is way near?

I see the trees swaying in motion
They begin to settle but then they
Pick up rapidly again, soothing but rough

An image comes to mind of running
Through the rain as a child and the emotions
I felt each time it rained. The happiness, it brought me
To just play in the rain and dance till I could not dance
anymore.

I would come in after a rainstorm
And sit by my bedroom window and look
Out and see the crystal clear droplets of rain
Sitting on the window, streaking down in lines.

Drawing myself out of the past and back to reality
I realize the day has not changed. I now begin
To feel tired and unmotivated my emotions feel completely
drained

I look out the window and see it is still raining
As now I am 17 I see the rain sometimes
I just want to run and play. To just feel the raindrops
Fall from my face and hair on to the ground.

I want to feel my bare feet
Squish between the soaking wet grass
I want to sing and run till I can't run anymore.

A feeling of refreshment falls over my face
I realize that it's just a faded memory
So I just go back to staring out the window
With a smile of everlasting energy on my face.

My Thoughts Exactly

You know it's weird that some people can come in and out of your life, and you really don't stop to think about how that person has touched you're life in one way or another. You end up walking away with a better understanding of yourself, and who you are as a person in this world. You walk away with lessons learned some harder than others.

You may not know exactly why you met that person, but you know they have a purpose for being in your life. Sometimes we walk through life so blind to the good things, and the good people we have in our life. We often forget to tell people in our everyday lives how much we appreciate them until maybe they are not there. We don't stop to think how lucky we are to have people who care about us, and respect us for who we are.

We may not always understand why we feel the ways we do, but in the end it makes us a stronger person. We may walk away from someone we care about, but we do for our own good. We may get frustrated with a situation we are going through in a relationship, but then we realize it could be worse.

We learn lessons every day from people, its part of how we learn, and grow as an individual. We strive to make the best of every situation regardless of the outcome. We come to understand that love is sometimes not always a mutual feeling, but it never stops being unconditional. We may walk through life wondering why we experience the things we do?

Are our lives really written in the stars? Do we live each day as if it is our last? Do we really stop to think about all the good things in our lives? We will never fully understand why people act the way they do. We just accept them for who they are.

Sometimes in life you may be looking for the perfect person, and stumble upon imperfection, but if you look deep into their heart, and soul you might find something even better than perfection. We often walk through life with the expectation of perfection, but we often find less of that; shouldn't that tell us something about ourselves?

You may walk alone knowing the real you, but never really knowing anyone else because they are afraid to let you in, and break down there wall of security because they have lived that way for so long. Some people may be too smart for your own good. Some people may mean the best, and just not show it. Some people may care, but not know how to express how they are feeling. Some people may be communicating to you, but you don't realize it because you feel like they have closed you off to the real them. Some people walk through life afraid of love. Afraid of getting hurt and some others just don't care how others see them.

I have learned several lessons as an individual the hard way. I have learned to love, and be there for people regardless of my feelings toward them. There is one thing I have learned and that is life is too short to waste on hatred toward others. I have also learned that you cannot change a person no matter how hard you try. They have to be able to love themselves enough to want to change to better themselves. Also you can't help them if they are not willing to help themselves.

No relationship or friendship is worth saving if someone gets mad at you for things that happen that are beyond your control. The simple answer to that is they need to find out who they are, and what they want out of life, before they can communicate and interact in a true relationship. People need to be able to love themselves before they can love anyone else.

You choose to live your life the way you want it. Live your life so you make it count. I believe anything you do in life should come from the heart. If you believe in yourself you can do anything, even if you feel like no one else believes in your dream it's your dream and you can prove to everyone you can do it. I am in a constant battle of people asking why? I simply reply because this is my dream and I want to do it. I want to make a difference in someone's life.

Often times I feel it's wrong to care, but it's how people perceive things. Challenge yourself to live your life to the fullest no matter what anyone else says. Reach for the stars. No matter who you are, you have a dream inside of you just waiting to be accomplished waiting to be discovered. Don't be afraid you are going to be rejected a million times in your life, and it is only going to make you a stronger person.

Stand up with a smile on your face, and a positive attitude in your heart. You will get further in life when people start to recognize you for who you really are, and the accomplishments you have made so far. Rather than the person they just assume you are.

September 11th 2001 – A Day That Changed the World Forever

Can't possibly describe how I am feeling now
It's like someone has put a blindfold over my eyes
I just stare at things hoping to find some answers to them.
Blindfolded to the world so many emotions just boiling
inside just waiting to bubble over
Not understanding what is happening around me and why?
Why all this chaos?
So many lives touched so many lives ruined so many lives
lost so many lives changed this is such an unspeakable
tragedy!
Not wanting to be away from the people I care about. It only
gives me a greater appreciation for the ones I love and care
about.
Feeling lost as if it's a dream, the world shattered in a million
pieces But yet it's real it's the truth we are dealing with as a
nation, but you just want to close your eyes and hope this
was all a bad dream.

So many lives touched not enough spared. So many true
heroes putting their lives on the lines, to help a country in
need. More than enough help but not nearly enough time to
save all those people's lives.

Just looking at the images brings tears to my eyes and makes me appreciate being alive. I was in my dorm room when the twin towers were hit that day it was almost as if time stopped. I could tell you everything that was said to every person I was with that day down to what I was wearing. It was one of the most horrific moments of my life that I will never forget. It makes me thankful for everyday I am here on this earth. I cherish it and think of it as a gift from god. Taking a look around me, and my life realizing how relieved I am that I had not lost a loved one or family member in all of this, my thoughts and prayers are with all the families who have to deal with the date year after year.

Looking back at images on TV they are so real so shocking so visible you can see the blood, the sweat, the tears, the scars, the disgrace, the dismay on people's faces on this country no doubt. Looking at the city the way it was, and now there is nothing left of the sky line that once stood so proudly but rubble and lifeless dead bodies, and proudly out of rubble the cross with the American flag letting us know that this country will go on and we will not give up without a fight until we take the 9/11 terrorist Bin Laden down.

The Wind

It can carry your spirit
Renew your senses
Refresh your soul
Capture what is inside of you
Add an iridescent touch of flavor to free your mind
Illuminate who you truly are
Express yourself ever so carefully
Be anything but the ordinary
Be bubbly
Don't forget to shine
Glitter with hope

Fall Mornings

Your flirty side
Love always who you are and what you're meant to be
You have the right to be fearless but most of all fabulous
Remember you like to be tied up but it's okay to never be
tied down completely
Be beautiful to yourself inside and out
Always think you're hot to trot
love and abide by the rules
But be a rebel
Get over it and embrace the new

Jennifer Meskun

Moves for Her

Boy friends
Girl smiles
What are you doing tonight?
You love us
Light love
You boy stuff

Don't Hide

The real you
Have more than one good side
Say what?
Don't be a statistic
Be strong
Love yourself enough to want to live

Smile

Why?
Ambition
You know that one word that completes a dream
Here is another
Optimism it powers a dream
Life is so complicated enough
Don't you have the right to be you think about it?
Shine on

Be Yourself

Bring out your beautiful side each and every moment of
every day
Meet the real woman behind the scenes
The one you have to see to believe

She's Come Undone

There is a certain disheveled coolness to the uniqueness she
possesses
Clothes with shattered tears
Holes in jeans
Raw edges
What if you ruled the world?
What are you wearing?
I just got to have these shoes
Stuff you can't live without
Isn't life just so juicy?

Advice

I love that fact that he knows that certain something
My almost favorite everything
I have so many crazy layers
I am uniquely qualified to take on your world
Things are never too sticky in my life
Sometimes the truth hurts for me and other people
Anxiety is a wasted Emotion
Comfort is always the bottom line
Some of the most beautiful people in world love others
He wants to
Love you

A Secret Place

There is a secret place only I know where I am going.
It is a place so peaceful so calm.
It is a place for me and my one true love.
It is a place to think my troubles through.
It is a place where images seem so real.
It's a place far off in the distance.
It is a place I can feel connected to.

Acceptance

I woke up today and I loved myself.
I loved the way I looked.
I loved the way I felt.
I wondered if it was just mirror image or a picture perfect
dream but whatever it was I felt good.

I felt free of worries
I just felt like being me.
I really liked who I was today
I could not figure it out
But with a little thought I finally figured out . . .

I accepted myself,
I accepted who I was and what I was all about,
I even accepted my flaws today,
This was hard for me to overcome at time.

I really understood where I was coming from
I had a more mature outlook
Not just small things but on life as a whole itself.
I felt as if I had the power to
Achieve anything I wanted to.
I felt as if I knew what I wanted
And was happy with myself,
And I was not going to let anyone stand in the way.

I had goals I wanted to reach
And I realized I could not reach them
With people constantly pulling me down.

I realized what was important
To me, and that I did not want to set
Those dreams aside from anything else.

I decided that the true key to happiness
Came from within no one else could
Prove it to me I had to prove it to myself.

Dreams

Never losing sight of a dream
I have come this far
I have accomplished so many goals so far
I only have more time to continue along with my journey

Losing some but gaining so much
Taking steps to become a more experience learner
Wanting to look back but I have so much more to offer
myself looking into the future
Seeing the potential I have and the insights I have to offer
other people

Finding once and a lifetime friends
Finding others that teach your lessons and then walk away
Finding within myself a tough soul to be able to stand the
obstacles obstructing my view and holding me down

Looking to myself for answers
Searching within to find the positive things that I have in my
life
Looking for that one thing to make me complete
Look to the ones you love to help support you

Sometimes in life you make choices to benefit you rather
then what your heart is telling you to do
Sometimes you need to listen to your intuition and let your
heart follow your head
Your heart will let you know what you are feeling, just go
with your instincts.

Sometimes in life we leave people behind
But we do not ever forget about them or the memories we
shared with them
We don't forget how they touched our lives in one small way
or another
We don't forget how they inspired us and allowed us to show
that side of ourselves we rarely show to anyone

We never forget the day the made us smile, the day they
made us cry, the first kiss we shared with them, the last kiss
we shared with them, the first time we looked into each
other's eyes or the first time we said I love you to them

We don't forget how they made us feel good about ourselves,
they made us feel bad about ourselves, we never forget how
they made us smile, or told us how beautiful we were. We
never forget how they told us that they loved everything
about us and we never needed to change a thing.

We never forget how someone knew you so well they could
tell your every thought or action.
We never forget all those talks we had about life and
ourselves. We never forget when they look into your eyes
they felt a truth so deep there were no words to put to how
that made their mind explode. We don't forget how they
touched our heart so deep that it was almost breath taking.

My True Self

Talking about life with you
Talking about my dreams
Seems to me you completely understand the way I view
things in my life
You feel how people affect me in my daily interactions with
them
You just understand what it is like to have a gift of caring for
people

Reciting my poetry to you is opening a door for me I rarely
open to anyone
You have seen my soft side like no one has before
You have found a way to my heart by finding what my
passion is in life: People
I believe that people make the world go round
Meeting people who touch my life in some way or another is
a gift all on its own
You have made me believe that there are people who share
the same interests you just have to find the right ones

The compassion we share for people
Goes beyond just how we view others
It's how we see those people
It's how we feel about changing their lives
Making them see and understand there is people out there
who care and would love to help

Hearing in your voice the determination towards your dreams and goals
Just believe things are going to fall into place isn't that what they always say
I believe it comes from within, you just know in your heart
you feel it, it won't go away it is like a fire burning so deep so fierce that you just won't let it go out

Seeing and inspiration in you, seeing insight into a field that never gets enough credit, a person who has the potential to go anywhere.
My goal is to get people thinking, to laugh, and bring joy to their day
If I am doing that then I have completed my mission in life

Smiling, positive attitude, upbeat those are the ingredients to life
Taking steps to make yourself known . . . well that will only make you more respected
Life throws curve balls your ways for reason
I believe you know sometime in your life maybe later on down the road
No matter what people come into your life for reasons and I believe you came into mine for a good reason to share your compassion for people with me.

You have sneaky ways about you that can even be a hidden
attraction
Sneaky ways build character
Character is your destiny
It so real and alive it's not a mirror image
It's a person with real feelings
It's a person who know how to find a way to a girls heart
A heart of gold and a mind of beauty the two put together
makes a complete scared soul. It's a kind heart and soul
feeling equals the compassion for one of life's more precious
gifts: PEOPLE

Reflection

I look through the window
Staring back at me is your reflection
Many thoughts enter my mind?

Scattered images
Pieces and parts
Time frames
Old memories

I just wonder what is buried so deep beneath that wall
That rough but at times gentle surface you call your life
Seeing broken shadows of lost love but seeing a whole new plan
A whole new world is developing inside your already
complicated fragile mind frame

Seeing confidence but upon closer examination I sense
something a pure cover up for fear
I am curious if your so called happiness has been marked by
your past histories.
You faintly remind me of people of my past and present life a
few unsure and a few unsettles
But yet you remain that unknown mystery to bother my soul
on a completely normal basis.

Somewhere inside your maze of self amusement there is a path leading to a world of so much more that nobody even knows about. You keep the real you hidden from the rest of the world. You don't want us to know the truth about you.

Are you human?
Just like the rest of us do you feel?
Do you have emotions?

I understand you have to maintain this certain game face from everyone today. This is true this is how society is. This is how people are. It's a dog eat dog world out there. You are on your own to fend for yourself.
If that means shutting people out of your life . . . I understand that comes first . . . Who cares about you? It's all about being protected!!
So my question is: are you afraid of yourself?
The innocent by stander always gets shut out by the wall it is indestructible.

Leader

I am a leader
One who stands up for myself
One who stands up for what I believe in

One who believes in gaining respect
Putting other people's needs before her own
Helping other people is my passion for life

How do you find a way to a girl's heart?
Lead with people
But don't abuse the power of her kind ways

She is a real person
Not just a changed image
You want her to be.

Have You?

Have you ever sensed or felt something
And it just seemed so real or present at the moment?
Have you ever took a leap of faith and never looked back?
Have you ever asked a question but did not ask why?
Did you ever sit down and take the time to ask yourself if you were selfish?
Did you ever feel some emotion but could not explain it so you held it captive in a secret place hidden away from the outer world?
Have you ever walked out the door and thought what if I don't come back today?
Have you ever thought about love in its truest form of the word?
If we did not have love for each other what would we have?
Did you ever wonder why people meet and come into our lives what are the reasons?
Have you ever just had enough and wanted to end it all?
Have you ever stepped outside your box your comfort zone and become your own person not what anyone else wanted you to be?
Are you afraid to take risks?
Do you walk a fine line in life?
Do you know when to have fun?
Do you know when to walk away and say this is not good for me I am not doing this anymore?
Do you know your balance in life?
Have you ever thought about your boundaries in life?
What do you value most in life? What three things could you not live without?

Where do your emotions come from?

Do you hide your true feelings because you're afraid or you have been hurt so you close the door and shut everyone out? You have no heart no soul it's been ripped out stepped on trampled on and broken so you trust know one but yourself I've been there.

Do you ever want to rescue people from themselves?

Do you ever want to just save the world and feel if you had magic powers and a wand you could?

Do you ever want to make a difference and an impact and get frustrated trying to do it?

Do you ever just need someone?

Do you ever miss someone for reasons you can't explain?

Have you ever met someone who grabs you by the heartstrings and does not let go?

Have you ever smiled so hard your face hurt or laughed so hard you brought yourself to tears?

Have you ever met someone you could just talk to for hours and never get bored?

Have you ever met someone who made you excited about life? Who made you be happy to be who you were?

Have you ever met someone you just treasured so much because parts of them reminded you of yourself?

Have you ever been there just been in someone else's shoes? Have you ever stepped foot in their path?

Have you ever not said anything and regretted it on any topic?

Do you feel fulfilled in life? Do you sparkle like glitter when you think about your life?

Do you hold back and never say how you really feel?

Did you ever burn a bridge that turned out to be important? What was the worst mistake you ever made? What was the best thing you ever did?

Do you feel judged? Do you judge?

What do you want to see changed in this world? What do you want to change about yourself?

Do you have hope? What does that mean to you?

Do you have dreams/goals where are they taking you? What have you done for yourself lately?

Do you lie to yourself about your true feelings?

Do you walk away never knowing the real you because you're afraid to look in the mirror?

Where do you get your self confidence? How does that help you in life?

Did something impact your life that changed you as a person forever?

Bottled Emotions

Bottled up emotions
Flowing hastily like mad waves
Crashing against rocks

Frustrated to the max
Feeling as steamed as
The mirror after a shower

I explained myself
Till I was blue in the face
You still don't trust me
You hurt me like a
Razor cutting deeply into
The pores of my deepest
Layer of outer skin

You don't understand,
You can't seem to grasp
The concept of the truth
You see things how you want
To see them, you don't take a moment
To consider my darkest feelings
Toward you

You are the enemy running
Away from your own twisted world
You live in a shadow of your own
Fears and you expect people to worship
Your deceiving identity

Your mind is one track
You pretend to be someone
Who you're not, you don't walk alone
You never have, you never will

You make people happy but
Then tear down their hopes
Of ever succeeding at the relationship

I came to the realization
That I don't have to visualize how
I want it to be, I can and
 Will make it a reality

Don't blame others for your insecurity
You without a doubt
Know unwillingly you're not always right
Well you're wrong this time

You're willing to risk everything
Happiness and faded memories
Over such a small injustice
That you purely designed
In your head

I was an innocent bystander
Why can't you see that?
Are you blinded by your selfish ways?
Or your conceited mind?
Do you think about what you are saying or doing?
Or do you just react when the truth had been told a million times
You still don't see that I have nothing to hide

Why would I lie?
Do you think that I keep things purposely hidden from your naked eye?
Can't you see the truth in my eyes?
Eyes that are incapable of lying to you

Wanting to figure things out
But only to be disturbed by the haunting image
Of a love once there but no longer a feeling the love
We once felt for each other

Blocked by distorted thoughts
That sound in my mind
Pieces and parts floating
Thoughts in my head like clouds
So life less and light

Unsure of what to think
But wanting to feel complete again
Wanting to be happy

Staying focused on new things
Never wanting to redeem that conversation
That ruined a well rounded healthy relationship
Letting words flow with no meaning
Tear apart a dream come true
First love and now no love
Just regrets resentment of greater and lesser value

I was not about to put things off
Just because of you I am not going
To put things on hold because of love
I am still pursuing what I dreamed of and longed
To do for so long, to do my best
And not one individual such as you will hold me back from
What it is I want to do

Tell me now! I am at your discretion
You tell me but you must know I am
And will not walk away knowing that
I have not made my point or said my piece

So what changed?
When did our relationship become
Such a stress in this teenage world of wonder?
What happened to the mature individuals we once were?

I think we lost ourselves in our own stubbornness
We cared too much, we are too much alike
Don't you care about the memories and the thoughts?
We once shared?
Our relationship consists of love and hate war and peace
Sometimes it's like committing a useless crime.

This is pointless I do not understand this rage
Your doubt in me
Your lack of respect; what happened to the old you?
Damn it! I need you
I want you to want me
I just don't know what else to say
Do you??

Why are this chaos and craziness?
It's as complicated for you to see around thing
As a maze intertwines and winds
Around and through things

Winds rapid movement bustling through your hair
Clearing your real identify of who you are
I don't even know you anymore
I whisper to you
In your eyes
I see shear happiness but in your mind
I see a wall of destruction
Inner beauty ruined all because of your self-worth
Was working in reverse hurting the ones who truly
Love you for you and not anything else

You destroy the inner me
You want me to change to be perfect
Everyone has faults
But somehow you don't trust that

You overpower me with your thoughts
You inspire me but you frustrate me
To see the not real you
The image behind the real face
The mask that is hiding your inner beauty

Why can't you see the other side?
You can't you're too focused on making an informal decision
you're taking things you heard
And making judgments

Why can't you see I loved you?
Why can't you accept the things you can't change?

You can't see you're blinded
By false accusations
-TYPICAL REAL TYPICAL

Dr. King

If one day you could put yourself in someone else's shoes
If for one day we could see people are not perfect
If for day we could hear the voice of another person
If for one day we could hear that one voice

The one voice of breath taking and intelligent words
The power of one voice so strong that changed a world
A dream so closed to be accomplished
A dream so indescribable but willing to risk your life for

Feeling love for others without restriction without regret
Trying to spare the hurt and pain
Trying to get equal rights for everyone in the process being
punished
Feeling as if the belief you instilled in everyone was not good
enough

You wanted to make it a reality but you did not quite know
how
Wanting to fight for your rights and the rights of others
So determined so close but your life was cut short because of
your determination
Feeling loved by so many individuals but hatred got in the
way of making a difference

The words flowed from your mouth like poetry you touched
so many lives
Why was your life not spared? Why were you the one who
was trying to promote goodness had to suffer? How come
you were understood by so many but misunderstood by so
many at the same time?

You longed for that day you worked so hard for
But you never got to see it
Don't worry your work did not go unnoticed
You're a hero to many in this nation including me

Your famous words "I HAVE A DREAM" inspired so many
people
You brought out the good in people
You made them see the reality of their actions

The Essence

Capture the essence of life
Savor the moment of contentment
Move away from the fear
Step out of the box
Face challenges head on
Clear your head long enough to understand
Simply the your stress
Free your soul
Reach your goal
Find the hidden truth
Unlocked the scared love
Make a statement
Be bold but endearing
Be kind not shallow
Breathe easy rest hard
Work hard rejoice in the payoffs
Make choices be clear
Love life
Be strong
Know right from wrong
See your inner beauty
Be a saving grace
Rejuvenate your spirit
Bask in your glory
Seal your fate
Take chances
Believe in yourself
Succeed with praise
Ask for help

Don't be jealous
Don't have resentment
Life is not a competition
Welcome change
Look at your heart
Remain the same
Be real not fake
Check the time it's never too late
Say I love you
Catch someone off guard
It's never too late to go too far
Light a candle
Inspire
Have hopes and dreams
Have values and means
Ask questions even it seems not important
Gentle eyes
Loving glow
It just makes my words flow
Dancing in my dream and always on my mind
It completely helps me to pass the time
Thinking of your smiling eyes

Inner Beauty

Look inside yourself
Unlock the key to you really are
Your beautiful inside
So pure so whole
I have this emotional glow
I feel free just to be me
I like who I am
Accepted for what I am and what I stand for
Love nourishes my soul
Make up accents my natural self
I am powerful in my own mind
I am driven and motivated

The Many Sides of Elaine

Elaine was a sophisticated young woman
She had a many of thoughts on her mind
And carried many dreams in her heart
She had a heart of gold
A spirit so free
A personality of 15 people let's say

Elaine liked to fool people
She liked to see what reaction she could get out of them
Everything from her eye color
To her hair color was up for grabs with her

Your never knew from day to day
Which Elaine would be walking in the door?
That was the mystery of her the shadow that smoked
everyone

Elaine was a house wife
Elaine was a nanny
But by trade Elaine was a bit of a comedian
That was Elaine's own personal little quirk you see

Elaine had many things up her sleeve
She wasn't your sheepish kind of gal
She loved to make people smile and if she could fool any
crowd she would

Jennifer Meskun

Elaine likes to be a spy she hides out in the crowd
Dresses up as other people
Wear disguises
Elaine is the master of all personalities

Elaine decided one day she got tired
Of her short hair she wanted a way
She could have instant curly hair, and the same if she wanted
long straight or
Highlighted or just a different color in general.
What was a girl to do without spending a fortune?

Elaine looked in to it
Dug deep down into her soul
Looked into her bag of tricks
And pulled out her bag of most useful tricks yet
Her heads of wigs
Elaine was going to be the next wig personality sensation

She had every kind wig you could imagine: for the full on
hair wigs she had: Brown hair longs curly, brown short
haired, brown highlighted curly, straight brown, and black
with red highlights.
She had clip ins—straight brown hair blonde hair blonde
curly hair
She had the pony tail clips—brown curly hair short and long
She had all sorts of ones you wrap around the bun in your
hair-brown, dark brown, medium brown
Last but not least she had extensions—blue and pink clip-ins

With Elaine it could be any day of the week
You never knew which personality you were getting
That was one of Elaine's best kept secrets
Boom she would keep quiet
Then one day slowly she would emerge
With one of her personalities and shock everyone

Elaine had a wild imagination
So did her under cover world
The wigs the make up the whole sense of style
She felt like a whole new person
That is why they call her the person with the 10 different
personalities

FEB 11TH 3:27 AM

Be vulnerable
Let your emotions flow
Let me see the real you
Come from behind the wall you hide behind
Experience your emotions without protection
Be real with me be one on one
I want to see your soul
Not the super hero mask you wear
Show me that shinning light that is there
So much hope inside its beautiful
You burst with positive beams
Goodness flows from the heart
Why hide that?
Show the world what you can do
The difference you can make

FEB 12ᵀᴴ 12:38 AM

My brain never stops processing . . . .
I feel like Sarah Jessica parkers role on the Sex and the City
The columnist who writes about the
Sex instead I am writing about my life . . .

It's a habitat maybe
I should just blog it
But be sure to save all my work and not lose any of it
After all this getting up in the middle of the night having
these thoughts
I also love to refer to myself in the third person

I scan through the thoughts
All jumbled in my head
Words just flying around everywhere
Parts and pieces to poems here and there

Scattered information
Time consuming
Note taking
Multitasking
Therapy sessions
Comic relief kind of like a Seinfeld episode if I could only
write my own and star in it
Serious conversations
Strong feelings
Disappointments
Anger

Our World

Smile
Be happy love life
Cherish the people you love
Be grateful
Bring joy to someone's life
Remind someone there worth it
Make someone feel special
Never give up
Think positive
Be the highlight of someone's day
Don't forget to laugh
Be real there is no need to hide
Give always
Go into things without expectations it is a lot easier
Give yourself a break
Don't beat yourself up
Don't assume anything in life

Stop gossiping it will save your life
Without your health you have nothing
Take nothing personally people live in their own worlds
I say let your inner child come out and play

Actions

I don't understand your actions
Your selfish ways annoy me
Do you know what you want?
What is going on in that mind of yours?

You can't be honest about how you feel so you try and hide it
I feel something is wrong but trying to break through your wall
Is quite the accomplishment
You have such potential but don't apply yourself—why is that?
What are you trying to hide from me just tell me the truth I
will be there to listen

What are you doing? Why are you acting so different?
You act one way one day and the rest day you're in a different
mode I never know with you
You anger me in so many ways you just walk away from
people who care about you
You try to look for people who give you some undivided
attention you are longing for

I am sorry I am not perfect but I do care and that should
count for something shouldn't' it? Why do you look at me
with such good intentions and act so selfish?
What are you searching for in your life to make it complete?
Are you searching for someone or answers you know you will
never find?

I used to know you and I don't know who you are anymore
I don't even want to begin to try to figure you out
You are a smart person you could have anything in this world
you wanted
You just make some wrong choices and moves

I need to do what I need to do for myself
If I need to walk away from you then so be it
I can't try living your complicated thought process
Your idea of communicating is not talking
How am I ever supposed to understand you if you don't tell
me how you feel?
Am I supposed to play guessing games I don't think so grow
up!

You walk in this world with a mind frame of perfection
Can't you just relax and enjoy the simple things in life
Or do you feel overcome by all the obstacles you are faced
with?

What is your problem? Why are you acting as if you don't
care about anything?
Is this your way of feeling accepted? Well you are passing by
people who really care about you and the things you do

Feeling frustrated by your heartless attitude
What happened to you the one who used to smile and laugh?
Why all of a sudden do you want to walk away from
everything we shared?

Why the grown up attitude all of a sudden? You are serious?
But this is a much greater feeling a feeling get that you are
not going to be happy till the problem is solved Do you
know you can't save the world?

You know you are only hurting yourself
Your moods kill any chance for conversation
Angered by your unforeseen ways
You are such a complicated individual
I feel bad for anyone who falls in love with you

You don't understand what you do to people
You take their friendship for granted so you will never set
yourself up for any kind of disappointments
Why do you go living your life as if you don't' care how you
affected by other people

It's funny that I think so much of you
I wanted to reach out a helping hand
But do you really care or are you just taking advantage of
people?

I don't understand the change you were so different when I
met you
I guess I didn't know the real you
I see through you, you can't lie
Most people would not put up with you but I do because I
care about you

You make me feel like it's my fault but it's not all in your
hands
You act professional toward higher authority and then when
it comes to your friends you don't think twice about how you
treat them

Maybe you should look around and see how your friends
like your hardheaded attitude. You think it is wrong to
express how you feel? Are you scared of rejection? You will
be rejected a million times in your life before you become a
stronger individual

What do you want from me? I am sick of playing head games
Just be honest I am not walking away till you tell me what is
on your mind
Why won't you let me be there for you? What are you afraid
of? I am not going to walk away from you. I will be there for
you not matter what the situation is I promise you that

Annoyed

Feeling annoyed by everything
Not really knowing why
Wanting to find an answer
But not really sure what the answer will mean

Feeling angered by your selfish ways
Walking way not wanting to cause a scene
I kept it to myself trying not to let it out

You only care about yourself
You don't care about others just what you want
You don't care who you're hurting
Or who it is in your way
It's all about you—that is all it ever is

You live in your own world
A world where you assume everyone likes you
Little do you know what people say behind your back
My heart goes out to you every time I think of the things

You try to get respect but you never will the way you are going
You are hiding behind your own identity
You're fake because we see what is
You think you will get respect
You make me look bad
I had to cover things up for you next time do it yourself

Jennifer Meskun

You think you're better than everyone else
You really don't think before you do things
You are too immature to see the things you do
You portray yourself as being innocent but people see right
through that

I have never seen such a person play games the way you do
You really like to mess with people's heads
It's not a game people have emotions

You try to interfere with others people's happiness
You can't find your own because you can't be happy
You're running away from your own twisted world of what
you call relationships

Why do you want to take away all that other people have
built upon?
Why can't you do things yourself?
Why do you depend on other people to do the work for you?

You have been spoiled all your life
You never had to lift a finger for yourself
Well welcome to the real world not everything is going to be
handed to you
Didn't someone ever tell you don't play with fire? You're
going to get burned

Emotions

Twisted emotions running through my mind
Not knowing what to think anymore
Trying to hold it together
But inside I feel like my guts are being ripped out

You said Honesty is key
Now you don't trust me that hurts
That hurts a lot

Pouring my heart out to you
You just sit there in complete silence
Not an emotion in mind
Tears streaming down my face
No words of comfort just silence
Not talking that is your way

Expressing every word to you
Trying to get you to understand
Telling you to everything I know
And you still don't trust me at all
I would not lie to you and
You're still angry

Jennifer Meskun

I never meant to hurt you
It was a huge mistake
Forgive and forget
What do you want?
When will you know?

I can't do this anymore
It's tearing me apart
Why don't you understand?
I LOVE YOU

Your Smile

Seeing that smile on your face
Makes me see that everything is going to be alright
Sometimes not knowing what to say but your smile assures
me it's going to be alright

I see things in you that no one else sees
I see the respect you have for me and I can't tell you how
much that means
I like how you reach out a helping hand you just always
know what to say

You're so strong in many ways it really amazes me how you
do it
You inspire me every step of the way and I can't thank you
enough for that
You can always make me smile no matter what mood I am in

Feeling a distant closeness almost like a form of trust towards
you
Not feeling certain on how things will always be I just
appreciate the time I spend with you now
Taking the time to do thing for me makes me see that there
are people who are not just selfish
Walking away with lessons learned and things that will help
me become a stronger and better person
Gaining insight and knowledge with every conversation we
have

Not wanting things to change but feeling a change. See confusion in your eyes maybe some type of not what to do or how to feel about a situation
Wanting to help but knowing you need time for yourself

Trying to understand you but getting frustrated with your indestructible walls
Looking from the outside in I see someone so smart and so logical
I would give anything to have what you have
I see a work of art, a doll
A person of perfection
Do you ever take a minute to see things for yourself? To not have to explain to anyone to just do thing for you that make you happy?

Learning about myself at the same time makes me wonder how I could do it, how I could take things so seriously, and not take time for the simple things in life.

Hidden Truth

Looking into your eyes I see a hidden truth
A truth so real it hurts
A love to be found with time
Hard to admit to yourself how you really feel

Letting a smile come across my face when I think of you
I just simply know my place in your heart
I miss you when you're not around to make me smile

Loving you for you sometimes is hard but I realize how
special you really are
Wanting to feel your sweet embrace wanting to be in your
arms
You always know how to make me smile no matter what
kind of mood I am in

You always say I worry too much your right I do
I think it s kind of funny how you always know what to say
That is why I can't stay mad at you for very long
I can't help but when I look at you I start to laugh when I get
like that you just know me so well
You put up with my layers so wonder you survived the true
test of friendship my personality
Your always there when I need you could have walked away a
number of times but you continually stayed by my side

We have not had the easiest time being friends if you even
want to call it that, but someone how we always resolved to
have a friendship in the end. We laugh hard and we taught
one another that we could be happy if we tried hard enough
We made it through some tough times and we have come out
stronger people

When I look at you I see something I can't explain
I just know how I feel
So hard to see past your wall but if I look deep in your heart
and soul I will find the answers I am looking for.

Your Mind's Eye

What is going on in your mind
When you're sitting here thinking
To yourself what you always dreamed things would be like

Everyone has dreams and visions
In their mind of a love so true
We all to have that prince charming
Come in and sweep us off our feet

Some of us wait so patiently
Because they know
It's not there time yet

Something get twisted
When there are so many emotions inside
And you need to come to some sort of conclusion
For yourself just to put your mind at ease
And satisfy that certain hunger that keep raging in your mind

You wonder how things got so crazy
And you wonder and are willing to do what it takes to make
things real again
You replay the memories you two shared

You want to speak out
You want to say what is on your mind
But you're afraid they won't feel the same way

Feelings are there
But the timing is wrong
You can run but you can't hide the fact the feelings are still
there
You're scared that it might be something good again
You don't want to make the same mistakes as before

Holding on but not as much as before
Undecided not knowing really if this is what you want
Or you just dreamed of it happening for so long and now
That it is here you don't know how to set it free and move on
to new horizons

When you look at the relationship
It's like a mirror image
So real but so far a reflection
You wonder is it too far faded.

Life

Sometimes life is not always easy
You live and learn that is the way it is
Sometimes you're e not even sure in life

Nothing is going to make perfect sense
You have to stick it through things could always be worse
You can wake up and be thankful of what you do have in
your life

Love will see you through no matter what happens
Things in life don't always go according to a plan
You will make it through just look at the individual you are
and the people around you who care
Look at the relationships that you have enjoy them walk
away smiling from the experiences you learned from them

No one said life was easy sometimes you have to move on
Sometimes we say things we don't really mean
But sometimes we leave things left unsaid till it is too late
Tell people how you feel when you are feeling it so they know
Even if it does not seem like people really appreciate you they
do on their own time

You may have dreams so far out of reach but there not so go
for it
Everything in life you should do should come from the heart
that is what I always say just give it your best and see what
happens

Don't forget the truth hurts and sometimes there is nothing you can do about it at least you know you were honest with yourself and others
Don't forget things in life happen for reasons

Sometimes in life you may be looking for the perfect person and you may stumble upon imperfection but if you look deep into that individual's heart and soul you might find something even better then perfection

We often walk through life with the expectation of perfection but we often find less of that shouldn't that tell us something about ourselves???

There are those people that come into our lives leaving an impact so strong that nothing or no other individual could ever replace them or the memories you had with them. Sometimes things don't work out despite the unbelievable connections we seemed to have had with people that is all part of life you gain some you lose some. In most situations you gain more perspective than anything.

Looking and searching for the perfect time to make things right again.
If you could turn back time you would
You would take it all back and just be friends you can't so now you're left with empty thoughts
You want to talk to them but you don't want to put yourself through all that again
You are often torn because it will make you happy but you are unsure of how you might fall again.

You can't take a risk like that again. You have worked so hard to better yourself and you have made something of yourself. You have come so far you put your heart and soul into all you have tried to achieve. So who can be disappointed with u?

You take a step back and imagine what you want your life to be like. You want to live a life free of hurt, pain and disappointment. You want to be happy you want to smile like you have not a care in the world

You look at what you have in life now and you would not want it any other way but still a part of you wants what you used to have but you sometimes have to move on and you can't go on living in the past.

Impressions

Walking away without a thought in mind
Not thinking a thing just walking away with a smile on my
face
The wind blowing across my face putting a chill down my
spine
The sun shines across the shimmering snow

Memories come back to me like last week's news
Lasting impressions good and bad
Words that were said I will always remember
A feeling of happiness comes over me

Snowflakes fall from the sky in every direction
Just reliving my childhood as I used to go and run in circles
as the snow would fall down around me
Playing and laughing letting all my problems flow free from
inside of me

Dreams come to mind
Wanting to live every moment to the fullest
Letting my imagination run wild
Letting every emotion that I have inside me be released
Feeling simply what is in my heart and nothing less of that

Letting my heart do all the talking
Feeling what I feel
Letting go of the grudges and really appreciating what I have
in front of me
Caring till the end of time
Never giving up until the moment I stop trying
Believing what I truly believe and nothing is left unsaid

Feeling loved
Giving love
It's never the same in return it's better
Not knowing how to express things but feeling things
It's like a fire burning with no way to put it out
It's so mysterious it always makes you think
You wonder what is going on inside them but are scared to
want to help

Somehow you always know it will be alright
Something is someone's voice that reassures you everything is
going to be all right
Not knowing what to say except that you appreciate them
every day they are with you
You walk away with a warm feeling like you have been
embraced with true words from the hear

You just walk away knowing that in one way that person has
made some sort of difference in your life good or bad they
just did. They made you smile when you were down they
turned your world upside down.

Creativity

Create who you are
Write it out
Draw it out
Figure it out
Put the words together
Use a quote
Make a rhyme
Make the time
Find out who you are
Find out what you can create in this world
Put in on with lip-gloss remember the sparkle is always there
How about the makeup that certain eye shadow has that flare
Do it up with the hair cut
Don't forget the wig
Put in the highlights
It's all part of my biz
Buy the clothes
Must have shoes
Pink is in
Create happiness
Colorful pictures
Colored contacts
Frame it
Collage it
Scrap it
Put it in a poem
Shop it
Bring it on
Pictures

Places
People
Events
Markers
Crayons
Pens
Color it
Finger paint it
Think outside the box
Be a kid again
Be a free thinker
Be brave
Be bold
Hold on tight
Never let go

Steps

Do you one day dream of taking that step where you can be completely free?

Do you one day want your words or works of art of creativity to reach someone else emotionally to be there for them like an unspoken rule.

It just hits them and they know this one detail you wrote or made will change their lives forever.

You create the unwritten rule

You become the difference the power behind the face that soul behind that believer in everyone

Your making your own journey to your life as you go along you don't want any mirror images of past hardships just foundations of new inspirations or new beginnings new meanings to life.

Memories

I carry with me
All the memories
My heart carries all the salts from the wounds of the words
you said you can't replace
I came with my stones written with my life stories on them
The girl who has a story to tell everyone

Frustration

I feel like my life is spinning out of control
I feel like I don't even know who I am anymore
Feeling like I was ripped to shreds once more
I don't know how much more of this adoption process I can
take
It's weighting on me—big time
Now I am being punished because of the medication I am on
You're going to try to ruin the rest of my life for me; thanks
a lot
You have no idea what that does to me inside
This is the one thing I want more than anything, and you
could be the obstacle standing in my way
I can't let that happen; I won't let that happen
This is a huge power struggle and I have no control; I know
nothing and you are jeopardizing everything—how could you?
You don't care; it's not you or your life
This is my life, it's has been toyed with for a year already you
think you can toy with me some more my . . . emotions are
tired of being messed with
Some days I don't know why I really bother at all
This process seems so useless and just aggravating
I just want to pull my hair out and scream at the top my lungs
Why is this so frickin' hard; why can't this be easy why can't I
just have one like everyone else?
I feel so much hurt, so much pain it's so unbearable there
really are no words anymore
I am numb; I see them everywhere

In the news people killing them, and here I go through all this to get one; it's just not fair. Who makes the rules? Who decides this?

I just can't do this anymore it's such a false sense of hope for what—NOTHING

I am such a good person all my life and this is how I get treated unbelievable!!

I have everything to lose and you have everything to gain

I feel like I am fighting for my life and this is one thing that puts me on edge

My dream has always been to have a family that's the one thing I don't have everyone else does.